Bitterness

When You Can't Move On

Paul Tautges

New Growth Press
newgrowthpress.com

New Growth Press, Greensboro, NC 27401
newgrowthpress.com
Copyright © 2023 by Paul Tautges

All rights reserved. No part of this publication may be reproduced, stored in a retrieval system, or transmitted in any form by any means, electronic, mechanical, photocopy, recording, or otherwise, without the prior permission of the publisher, except as provided by USA copyright law.

Unless otherwise noted, Scripture quotations are taken from The ESV® Bible (The Holy Bible, English Standard Version®). ESV® Text Edition: 2016. Copyright © 2001 by Crossway, a publishing ministry of Good News Publishers. The ESV® text has been reproduced in cooperation with and by permission of Good News Publishers. Unauthorized reproduction of this publication is prohibited. All rights reserved.

Scripture quotations marked NASB are taken from New American Standard Bible®, Copyright © 1960, 1971, 1977, 1995, 2020 by The Lockman Foundation. All rights reserved.

Cover Design: Dan Stelzer
Interior Typesetting and eBook: Lisa Parnell

ISBN: 978-1-64507-325-3 (Print)
ISBN: 978-1-64507-326-0 (eBook)

Library of Congress Cataloging-in-Publication Data on file

Printed in India

30 29 28 27 26 25 24 23   1 2 3 4 5

In 2005, I struggled with bitterness. It began shortly after we went under contract on a big farmhouse in the country. After spending five years renovating our first house, it had become obvious that we had outgrown it. Five daughters were sharing one bedroom, and it was time to look for something that would be a better fit for our large family. We began searching for a few acres for our seven kids to roam. It didn't matter how much work the house needed; we just wanted some space. We sold our fully remodeled home and signed a contract on a large, dilapidated house on seven acres only ten minutes from our church.

Since the farmhouse was an income property for its owners, they told us they needed an extra month to find another place to put their investment capital in order to avoid taxes. "In the meantime," they said, "go ahead and close on the sale of your current house and move in." The owners were professing Christians, so we took them at their word. But as time passed, they repeatedly informed us they had not yet heard the voice of Jesus telling them to close the sale, but they were sure they would hear soon. We believed and hoped for the best.

Some of our new neighbors began reaching out with careful inquiry. "We should close any day now," we optimistically said, as they smiled and offered sympathetic words. We were confused, especially when we learned the previous purchaser-turned-tenant was strung along for ten years. After five months of waiting, we were forced to hire an attorney to draft a letter to the sellers insisting that they set an official closing date, but they ignored the letter.

Eventually, we fully awoke to the nightmare before us. We had been swindled. Not only that, but since we were naive and ignorant of the fact that a signed real estate contract can fall through, we had made other financial decisions based on the purchase-plus-renovation package our credit union had put together. In short, we were worse than broke. Our plans were wrecked and our ability to purchase another home was slim.

Once the dust settled, I started to become resentful. Anger against the sellers was justified. *They're crooks and liars! Worst of all, they did this to us while mentioning the name of Jesus in every other sentence!* My anger started out righteous—they were wrong and had treated us unfairly—but it went downhill from there. I was also angry at myself. *I'm a total idiot!* I thought. *Not only did I make an unwise decision that would affect my family for years to come, but I'm also a failure. I deserve this. What a loser!*

Deep down and unbeknownst to me, I was also angry at God. He should have kept this from happening to my family. I knew from Scripture that I wasn't in a good place and couldn't stay like this, but I didn't understand that my anger was feeding a distrust of God. I was not trusting him with my family, my future, or my feelings. I didn't know how to talk to the Lord about this injustice.

As a pastor, I frequently counseled others to hope in God and preached sermons on his sovereignty, but

I was having a hard time applying it to my situation. I had not yet learned from personal experience the truth of what Jerry Bridges expresses so well: "Bitterness arises in our hearts when we do not trust in the sovereign rule of God in our lives."[1]

I chafed under the faith-building regimen designed by my heavenly Father, and my response to this unpleasant experience only made matters worse. We had moved our belongings to another house, but my heart could not move on from how we had been mistreated. I was stuck, and all I could think about was the wrong committed against us.

It's only natural to bristle against mistreatment or unjust circumstances. An array of emotions—whether that be anger, frustration, or the like—are sure to rise to the surface when we are sinned against or when circumstances don't pan out the way they should. But when does our response slide from recognition of wrong to bitterness? Bridges again helps us by giving the following understanding of bitterness: "[It] is resentment that has grown into a feeling of ongoing animosity. Whereas resentment may dissipate over time, bitterness continues to grow and fester, developing an even higher degree of ill will."[2] This was certainly true in my case. Bitterness was growing and the garden of my heart was producing thorns.

Perhaps you can relate to one or more parts of my story. Perhaps not. Regardless, we are all tempted to become bitter about the painful trials we go through, or against people who mistreat us—whether intentional or not. What does bitterness look like in your life? Perhaps you picked up this little book because you've become resentful about being passed over for a job promotion, were hurt by a member of your church or family, were falsely accused or slandered, or were taken aback by a severe disappointment. No matter what your struggle with bitterness may look like, the Bible speaks truth and hope into your mind and heart.

My goal is to help you understand and apply the biblical principles the Lord brought home to my heart during my struggle with bitterness. I don't pretend to be immune to the subtle temptation for this sour attitude to grow back. However, when unwanted thoughts and negative emotions arise, I know how to deal with them. While I'm still learning to be more aware of the workings of my heart, I hope to spare you from going down the road I went down by learning from my failings, and those of others found on the pages of Scripture.

The Two Sides of Bitterness

The Bible reveals two categories of bitterness. The first explains *the bitterness of hard life experiences*, while the second exposes *bitter responses* to difficulties and the wrongs committed against us.

The bitterness of affliction

Inevitably, we will all face the painful realities of life in this broken world. This is the bitterness of affliction, and it has more to do with our outward circumstances than our response to it. Scripture is full of candid examples of this type of pain: infertility, betrayal, financial loss, oppression, and more. As you encounter adversities, it is helpful to be aware of what bitterness may look and feel like so that you may face affliction well.

Two words are most often used in Scripture to define and describe bitterness—one in the Old Testament and one in the New. The Old Testament uses the Hebrew word *marah*, which means angry, bitter, chafed, and discontent. It's used literally for water (Exodus 15:23), food (Exodus 12:8), fruit (Deuteronomy 32:32), and physical pain (Numbers 5:24). It's used figuratively for the bitter cry of Esau after he realized his brother Jacob had stolen their father's blessing (Genesis 27:34), times of mourning (Amos 8:10), and for Hannah weeping in prayer over her infertility (1 Samuel 1:10). The book of Job employs the word to describe the poisonous putrid bile from the gall bladder (Job 16:13; 20:25) or the poison of snakes (Job 20:14).[3] The comparison to poison highlights the polluting influence of bitterness in us and on those around us.

The New Testament employs the Greek word *pikros*, from the root meaning to cut or prick. It refers to a sharp, pungent sense of taste or smell (think of a ripe skunk on the side of the road). For example, James employs the word both literally for water and figuratively for jealousy (James 3:11, 14). As a verb, it means to be embittered against another person, such as a husband becoming bitter against his wife (Colossians 3:19). It may also describe the emotional pain of failure, like the intense grief of Peter who, after denying Jesus, "went out and wept bitterly" (Luke 22:62).

Together, these words portray bitterness as the opposite of sweetness. We see this vivid contrast in the book of Exodus:

> They went three days in the wilderness and found no water. When they came to Marah, they could not drink the water of Marah because it was bitter; therefore it was named Marah. And the people grumbled against Moses, saying, "What shall we drink?" And he cried to the LORD, and the LORD showed him a log, and he threw it into the water, and the water became sweet. (Exodus 15:22–25)

The Old Testament book of Ruth illustrates this contrast well. Its main characters lived in a period of political oppression and utter chaos. It was a time of spiritual apostasy as God's people adopted the worship and practice of the pagan Canaanites whom the previous generation had failed to "utterly destroy" as God had commanded (Deuteronomy 20:17, NASB). The "days when the judges ruled" (Ruth 1:1) were the dark ages of Israel's history—a bitter time when "everyone did what was right in his own eyes" (Judges 17:6).

In the first chapter, we meet a woman who endures much pain and loss. Her birth name is Naomi (meaning *pleasant*), but later in life she asks people to call her Mara, which means *bitter*. Why is that? What bitter tasting affliction brought such pain into her life? How did she get to this point? Before we rush to judgment, let's try to put ourselves in her shoes.

Naomi's affliction began when famine prompted her husband to move them and their two sons fifty miles east, from Bethlehem to Moab—from the land of promise to the land of pagans. While there, all three men died (Ruth 1:3–4). Before the sons died, however, they married Moabite women who were descendants of one of the incestuous unions of Abraham's nephew, and enemies of Israel (Genesis 19:37; 2 Kings 23:13). The lives of the three grieving widows were intertwined. Surely, they wondered what the future held.

So Naomi reversed the direction her family took ten years earlier. She turned her back on the three graves and made a clean break from the tragedy that had befallen them. On the way back to Bethlehem, she directed her daughters-in-law to return to their people, and pronounced a blessing of God's compassion on them (Ruth 1:8). One daughter-in-law returned to her parents and her gods while the other, Ruth, turned to the Lord and remained with her mother-in-law. As the two traveled home, Naomi's faith waned as her sorrowful heart became consumed by how "the hand of the Lord [had] gone out against" her (Ruth 1:13).

We all experience bitter tasting affliction and a host of other troubles and heartaches. What does your adversity look and feel like? Perhaps it is an unexpected turn of events completely outside of your control, like what Naomi endured, or the painful weight of personal failure. No matter the source, suffering has a way of revealing what we believe about God and his providential care for us. It can shape our perspective and make it difficult for our faith to embrace the reality that God is up to something good amid the bad.

Bitter responses

Bitter afflictions have the potential to distort our thinking and cloud our remembrance of the heavenly Father's love, faithfulness, and good purposes. As it was for Naomi, profound loss can cast a shadow over the eyes of our heart and leave us vulnerable to the temptation to resent God because life turns out different from what we expected. Therefore, we must grasp an important principle: *A bitter experience may produce a bitter spirit when we do not interpret suffering biblically or respond to it humbly.* This is the second category of bitterness: the bitter response which comes from our hearts. Naomi's response to her affliction illustrates three ways bitterness may steer you away from trusting in the Lord.

1. *Bitterness skews your view of yourself.* "Is this Naomi?", the women in town ask the one who perhaps now wears a worn-out, bitter countenance. "Do not call me Naomi; call me Mara," she said, "for the Almighty has dealt very bitterly with me" (Ruth 1:20). Naomi's self-talk sounds like this: *Call me Bitter, Angry, or Grieving. But don't call me Pleasant.* Bitterness has become more than Naomi's experience; it now defines her.

Bitter, with an uppercase B, is her new name. In the wake of her unspeakable loss, Naomi temporarily lost sight of how deeply Jehovah loved her and instead focused only on her pain. Are you ever tempted to do the same? When affliction is overwhelming, it's easy to let our past trauma or present suffering define us. For example, the pain of loss or the upset of a medical or psychiatric diagnosis may overtake our mind and encourage us to see ourselves only through a darkened lens. Perhaps you think your trial defines you, but that is not who you are. In Christ, you are loved beyond measure and have received a new name: Beloved child of God (1 John 3:1).

2. *Bitterness causes you to forget God's goodness.* Amid her affliction, Naomi's view of God became nearsighted. The "Almighty has brought calamity upon me," she testifies (v. 21). She lost her wide-angled view of the breadth of God's goodness, kindness, and purpose in all things. Now, she sees a God who has only brought horrendous pain into her life. *God is only against me. "Bitter" is now who I am.* But God hadn't turned away from Naomi. He was about to show her his love and care in the most amazing way.

Is this also happening in your life? Is bitterness about your current struggle giving you tunnel vision—obscuring your view of the ways you have experienced God's love, tender mercy, and provision?

3. *Bitterness exaggerates your suffering, thus blinding you from seeing God's character and trusting his plan.* Naomi interpreted her suffering as proof that God was against her. "I went away full, and the Lord has brought me back empty. Why call me Naomi, when the Lord has testified against me and the Almighty has brought calamity upon me?" (Ruth 1:21). In her pain, she could not see the blessing standing an arm's length away. *I went to Moab with a husband and two sons, and now I've come back alone!* But she was not alone. She had Ruth, a brand-new believer in Jehovah, with a tender heart of devotion. What a gift she was to the suffering Naomi! Yet bitterness grew cataracts over the eyes of Naomi's heart, thus preventing her from seeing God's mercy and provision. As the drama unfolded, neither woman knew what God was up to backstage—bringing good from bad. Unbeknownst to them, the suffering of one Bethlehem family would become the doorway through which the redemptive plan of God took a step forward. An older relative named Boaz redeemed the widowed Ruth, and the book ends with their infant son resting on Naomi's lap. Who is this boy? Obed, the son of Boaz and Ruth, the grandfather of King David, through whom was born Jesus our Savior (Ruth 4:17; Matthew 1:1–6). God certainly *was* up to something good!

Warnings Against Sinful Anger

In the Bible, the *heart* is the always-active, ever-worshipping, always-wanting-something control center of our lives. Therefore, when something or someone gets in the way of our desires and expectations, we are tempted to respond in anger. Then, if we allow anger to linger, we grow bitter, which hurts us and others. In the book of Ephesians, the Spirit warns against this response by reminding us of who we are as believers in Christ (Ephesians 4:1–24).

In Christ, you are dead to sin and alive to God because the Holy Spirit caused you to be born again by the power of the life-giving gospel. *Therefore,* you now have a secure standing before God and the indwelling Spirit to empower you to put off sinful ways and walk in the righteousness and freedom of Christ. It is in this larger context that God commands you to beware of misplaced, sinful anger. "Be angry and do not sin; do not let the sun go down on your anger, and give no opportunity to the devil" (Ephesians 4:26–27). In this verse, there are two warnings to heed.

Righteous anger may quickly become unrighteous

Anger is not automatically sinful and can be a godly, appropriate response to evil. For example, the Gospel accounts inform us that Jesus, the sinless Son of God, was angry (Mark 10:13–16; John 2:13–18). Nevertheless, for us, the line between righteous and unrighteous anger is extremely thin—it's easy, even natural, for us to cross over. In his book, *Uprooting Anger*, Robert Jones describes three distinguishing marks of righteous anger.[4]

1. *Righteous anger reacts against actual sin.* Righteous anger arises from an accurate perception of evil defined biblically as a violation of God's Word. Righteous anger does not result from merely being inconvenienced or from violations of preference or human tradition. It is provoked by actual, not imagined, wrongs.
2. *Righteous anger focuses on God and his kingdom, rights, and concerns; not on me and my kingdom, rights, and concerns.* God-centered—not self-centered—motives drive righteous anger. Righteous anger focuses on how people offend God and his name, not you and your name.
3. *Righteous anger is accompanied by other godly qualities and expresses itself in godly ways.* Righteous anger remains self-controlled. It keeps its head without cursing, screaming, raging, or flying off the handle. Nor does it spiral downward in self-pity or despair. It does not ignore people, snub people, or withdraw from people. Sinful anger gives people "the silent treatment." Righteous anger does not.

However, even if our anger passes all three tests, we must not remain there. "Do not let the sun go down on your anger" compels us to address our anger and its sinful expressions immediately. This implies that we work through our interpersonal conflicts as soon as possible, as Jesus also commands (Matthew 5:23–25).

Lingering anger grieves the Holy Spirit and gives the devil the opportunity to destroy

As we've already noticed, anger often stems from not getting what we want (James 4:1–10). This gives the devil opportunity to exploit our unmet desires by tempting us to remain discontent. If we linger there, we hand over some of the real estate of our hearts to Satan and become easy prey for the prowling lion to devour (1 Peter 5:8). This was the case with another Old Testament example, Esau, whose resentment produced a desire to murder his brother, and corrupted his heart further (Genesis 27:1–41). As it was with Esau, bitterness will turn you into a murderer—perhaps not by taking a person's life, but by destroying their spirit with harsh words or punishing them with silence. This sinful response grieves the Holy Spirit "by whom you were sealed for the day of redemption" (Ephesians 4:30).

Thankfully, the apostle does not leave us only with dangers to beware. He also gives a Christ-centered solution.

Apply the Biblical Remedy

As the fourth chapter of Ephesians ends, Paul exhorts us to action, to put feet to our new life in Christ by putting off bitterness and putting on grace: "Let all bitterness and wrath and anger and clamor and slander be put away from you, along with all malice. Be kind to one another, tenderhearted, forgiving one another, as God in Christ forgave you" (Ephesians 4:31–32).

Put away bitterness and all its unsavory relatives

Bitterness gives birth to a family of sins. In verse 31, the apostle introduces us to five disagreeable relatives: *wrath* (an outburst of passion, rage), *anger* (a state of hostility), *clamor* (loud shouting), *slander* (abusive speech that tears a person down—usually behind their backs), and *malice* (general wickedness). You must remove these from your life completely. Since bitter words flow from the fountain of a bitter heart (James 3:10–11), removal begins by confessing your sinful responses to God and repenting before others, when necessary. To change your speech patterns, you must notice what is going on in your heart. Learn to ask yourself, "What do I want so badly that I'm willing to commit murder in my heart to get it or keep it?" Yet, it's not enough to put away bitterness and all its unwelcome family members; you must also put on grace, which is illustrated in the next verse.

Replace destructive patterns with Christlike love and grace

While putting away bitterness and its sinful relatives, we must also put on Christian virtues like those mentioned in verse 32, being "kind to one another, tenderhearted, [and] forgiving." *Kindness* is doing good to others, especially those who wrong us, while *tenderheartedness* extends from mercy. Forgiveness, however, is the golden key to unlocking the self-made prison of bitterness. *Forgiveness* is letting go of offenses or putting them away, like God—who no longer holds our sins against us (Psalm 79:8). Forgiving others "as God in Christ forgave you" is the new standard for the believer; it is the trademark of the new self. Are you stuck? Are you struggling to let go of bitterness? Remember that God shows how deeply he loves you by sending his Son to save you (Romans 5:8). Realize how much Jesus wants to help you walk in the freedom that he purchased and be encouraged that the Spirit is praying for you (Romans 8:26). He who endured the greatest injustice of all—being punished for sins he did not commit—is also the One who left an example of how to respond when we are treated unfairly. "When he was reviled, he did not revile in return; when he suffered, he did not threaten, but continued entrusting himself to him who judges justly" (1 Peter 2:23). By handing over our injustices to the Judge of Heaven, we can let go of bitterness and walk in the newness of life. Will you entrust yourself and your hurts to the Lord who delights in you (Psalm 18:19)?

Check Your Heart

The New Testament contains a sober warning which connects the unrepentant pattern of bitterness to the unregenerate heart of the unsaved. Hebrews was written to a congregation largely made up of Jewish people who professed faith in Jesus. However, some had deceived themselves and, therefore, the author challenges all of us to check our hearts:

> Strive for peace with everyone, and for the holiness without which no one will see the Lord. See to it that no one fails to obtain the grace of God; that no "root of bitterness" springs up and causes trouble, and by it many become defiled . . . . (Hebrews 12:14–15)

Pursuing peace and practical holiness are marks of authentic conversion—proof that we are new creatures in Christ. Thus, quoting from Deuteronomy, the writer of Hebrews urges us to beware of "the root of bitterness," which refers to the idolatry of which some Israelites were guilty during their wilderness wandering. Bitterness is not only an expression of the old self, of which God commands us to repent, but may be symptomatic of a life that has failed "to obtain the grace of God." Jesus comes to the same conclusion in his parable of the unforgiving servant (Matthew 18:21–35).

On the flip side, however, the ability to forgive others who wrong us is evidence of God's grace active within us. Jesus fully paid for our sins and rose to give us new life: "For Christ also suffered once for sins, the righteous for the unrighteous, that he might bring us to God" (1 Peter 3:18). When he died in our place, the weight of sin which Jesus carried surely includes the heavy burden of bitterness. Therefore, he graciously invites us to bring our sin to him, as well as the hurt associated with the ways others sin against us. Jesus promises to carry our burdens with us: "Come to me, all who labor and are heavy laden, and I will give you rest. Take my yoke upon you, and learn from me, for I am gentle and lowly in heart, and you will find rest for your souls" (Matthew 11:28–29).

The shoulders that carried our sin and shame to the hill called Calvary are strong enough to also carry the sins committed against us. We can lay them down at the feet of the One who understands our need because he walked the same bitter road. Are you trusting Jesus in this way? Will you lay your burdens down at his feet? Ask Jesus to sweeten the bitter waters of your heart.

Coming Full Circle

One year after our fiasco in the country, we received news of the sudden death of the husband by heart attack. In the providence of God, we now "just happened" to live across the street from the funeral home where the service would be held. Immediately, my wife and I knew what we must do. As Christ followers, we knew what God expected from us. We walked across the street to actively put to death any lingering anger. We walked across the street because of how much God, in Christ, forgives us. We walked across the street to extend the love and grace of Jesus. For an hour, we visited with the recent widow and, in response to our prayers, received strengthening grace so that we could pass it on to one who had deeply wronged us.

In the months that followed, my wife and I were standing in our kitchen when the phone rang. It was the widowed property owner who called to thank us for coming to her husband's funeral. Then she said something that we never expected. She confessed she had recently come to realize how badly she had wronged us and was sorry for the distress she and her husband brought on our family. Immediately, we granted forgiveness. "We forgive you," I said. "We already forgave you in our heart, but now it brings us great joy to tell you. We believe the Lord is in control and, somehow, he will bring good out of it." Our heart wrenching debacle was over. It was a painful, but spiritually beneficial, lesson. Bitterness may be subtle. I didn't see its presence in my heart for many months. Thankfully, the Spirit graciously overcame my pride and broke through the outer crust of my hardening heart. He nurtured my faith, conquered my lingering anger, and restored me to others. What is your need today? What has the Holy Spirit unearthed in your heart?

Dig Deeper and Move Forward

If the Lord revealed any bitterness in your heart while reading this minibook, the following projects will help you apply what you've learned.

Learn to lament

One biblical discipline that I learned during my battle against bitterness is lamenting to God in prayer. Lament complains *to* God, but not *about* God. Mark Vroegop defines lament as "a prayer in pain that leads to trust. . . . It is the path from heartbreak to hope."[5] Biblical lament follows a four-step process: (1) turn to God, (2) complain to God, (3) ask God for help, and (4) choose to trust. Work through some Psalms of Lament, such as Psalm 10, 13, 22, 39, 44, or 77. Journal about how other believers followed this four-step process to work through their pain. Consider reaching out to a mature believer to ask them to walk through some Scripture with you.

Consider the vertical and horizontal dimensions of bitterness

Bitterness has vertical and horizontal dimensions. In Naomi's response to her affliction, we noticed some ways bitterness may affect our relationship with God. Additionally, in Ephesians, we learned to pay attention to how bitterness affects our relationship with others. Consider these connections further.

- Read Psalm 73:21–22. Asaph wrote this song after a season of bitterness and envy, which stemmed from comparing his agony to the relative ease of the wicked. Are you angry at God about your past or present? If so, confess this

to God by praying through Psalm 73:21-28 in your own words.
- Read Romans 12:14–21. Bitterness tempts us to act out in vengeance toward those who mistreat us, but these verses compel us to live in peace. Do you strive to live in harmony with others? Perhaps you can honestly say, "So far as it depends on me, I've done all I can to live peaceably with [insert name here]." If this is true, how can you pray for them and yourself? How can you guard your heart from recurring anger and nurture a forgiving spirit?

Pursue peace

In contrast to the relational animosity that often accompanies bitterness, faithful Christians "aim for restoration" (2 Corinthians 13:11). Bridges explains, "True forgiveness results in a restored relationship, not continuing animosity."[6] Who do you need to contact to initiate reconciliation?

Let go

Practice biblical forgiveness.[7]

- *Think:* Make a list of the experiences about which you are still angry. What afflictions are you disappointed with God about? Who do you harbor bitterness against?
- *Pray:* Confess any unbelief or sinful responses to the Lord. Pray for those who hurt you.

- *Let go:* Put your list through a paper shredder or burn it in a fireplace or grill. Destroy it as an outward expression of letting go of hurt and putting away all bitterness.

Life can be bitter. Unforeseen turnarounds and unspeakable sorrows have the potential to leave us feeling beat up and confused, thus preparing the garden of our hearts to become a seedbed for bitterness. But Scripture re-centers us; it realigns us with our loving God and his promises. His grace in Christ strengthens our inner person to accept his plans by faith and to forgive others so that we can move on.

Further Resources

Ernie Baker, *Help! I'm in a Conflict* (Wapwallopen, PA: Shepherd Press, 2015).

Robert D. Jones, *Freedom from Resentment* (Greensboro, NC: New Growth Press, 2010).

———, *Pursuing Peace* (Wheaton, IL: Crossway Books, 2012).

———, *Uprooting Anger* (Phillipsburg, NJ: P&R Publishing, 2005).

Michael Lawrence, *Conversion* (Wheaton, IL: Crossway Books, 2017).

Jim Newcomer, *Help! I Can't Forgive* (Wapwallopen, PA: Shepherd Press, 2016).

David Powlison, *Good and Angry* (Greensboro, NC: New Growth Press, 2016).

Paul Tautges, *A Small Book for the Hurting Heart* (Greensboro, NC: New Growth Press, 2020).

———, *Anxiety: Knowing God's Peace* (Phillipsburg, NJ: P&R Publishing, 2019).

Stephen Viars, *Overcoming Bitterness* (Grand Rapids, MI: Baker Books, 2021).

Mark Vroegop, *Dark Clouds, Deep Mercy: Discovering the Grace of Lament* (Wheaton, IL: Crossway, 2019).

Lauren Whitman, *A Painful Past: Healing and Moving Forward* (Phillipsburg, NJ: P&R Publishing, 2021).

Endnotes

1. Jerry Bridges, *The Pursuit of Holiness* (Colorado Springs, CO: NavPress, 1978), 122.

2. Jerry Bridges, *Respectable Sins* (Colorado Springs, CO: NavPress, 2007), 130.

3. Steven Viars, *Overcoming Bitterness* (Grand Rapids, MI: Baker Books, 2021), 13.

4. Robert Jones, *Uprooting Anger* (Phillipsburg, NJ: P&R Publishing, 2005), 29-30.

5. Mark Vroegop, *Dark Clouds, Deep Mercy* (Wheaton, IL: Crossway Books, 2019), 28.

6. Bridges, *Respectable Sins*, 131.

7. For a definition of forgiveness, which includes four promises, see Ken Sande's article "Biblical Forgiveness Enables You to Forgive as God Forgave You" at https://rw360.org/biblical-forgiveness/.